Religious Stories

The Life of the Buddha

John Snelling

Illustrated by
Carol Barker

Religious Stories

Buddhist Stories
Chinese Stories
Creation Stories
Guru Nanak and the Sikh Gurus
Hindu Stories
The Life of the Buddha
The Life of Jesus
The Life of Muhammad
The Lives of the Saints
Old Testament Stories

Editor: Stephen Setford

First published in 1987 by
Wayland (Publishers) Ltd
61 Western Road, Hove,
East Sussex BN3 1JD, England

British Library Cataloguing in Publication Data
Snelling, John, *1943–*
    The life of the Buddha. – (Religious
    stories series)
    1. Buddhists – India – Biography –
    Juvenile literature
    I. Title   II. Barker, Carol   III. Series
    294.3'63   BQ892
ISBN 0–85078–903–6

Phototypeset by
Kalligraphics Ltd, Redhill, Surrey
Printed in Italy by
G. Canale & C.S.p.A., Turin
Bound in the U.K. by
The Bath Press, Avon

Contents

Prince Siddhartha is born

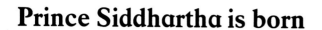

Lumbini was a place of lovely gardens. It nestled at the foot of the soaring Himalayan mountains.

There, about 2,500 years ago, a baby boy was born. He was the son of King Suddhodana and Queen Maya, who ruled a tiny kingdom in that part of India. They called their son Prince Siddhartha Gautama.

While Prince Siddhartha was still a baby, a wise man named Asita came to see him.

'What a marvellous baby!' Asita cried. 'There is a special sign on every part of his little body. This means that he will be a very great man when he grows up. He may become an emperor. Or he may even become a buddha – a wise teacher who will help people live happier and better lives.'

But then Asita began to cry.

'What's the matter, Asita?' King Suddhodana asked.

'I am crying because I am old,' Asita explained. 'I will probably not live long enough to hear the wise and good things your son may have to say if he grows up to be a buddha.'

King Suddhodana was very unhappy when he heard what Asita had said. The King did not want the Prince to leave home and become a buddha. He wanted Siddhartha to stay and become king when he grew older.

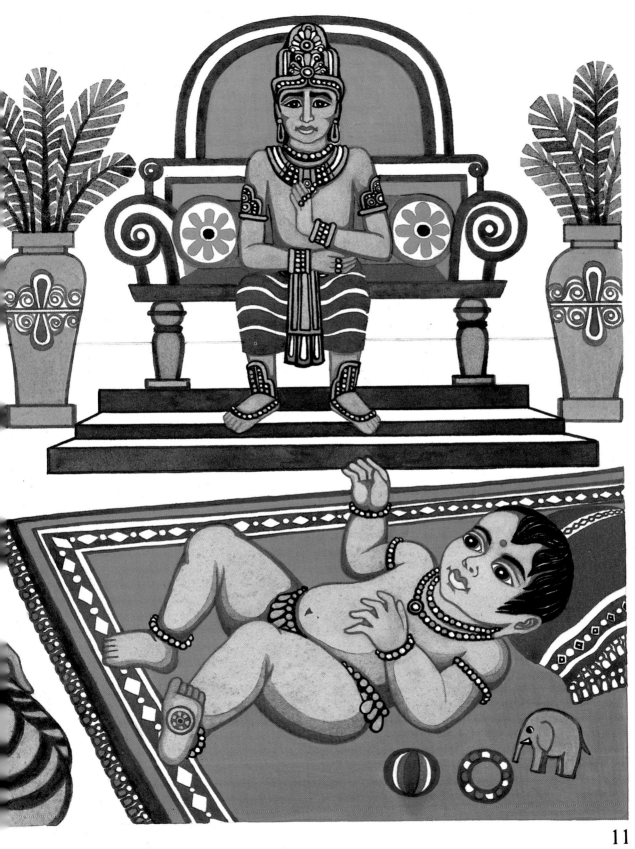

'I know what I'll do,' King Suddhodana said after thinking the matter over. 'I'll build him three splendid marble palaces. Everything in them will be new and beautiful. There'll be all sorts of toys and games to keep the Prince happy.'

'He'll have only the tastiest foods to eat and only the smartest clothes to wear. All his servants and friends will be young and healthy too, so that he will not find out about old age, sickness and death. Then he'll never want to become a buddha.'

13

14

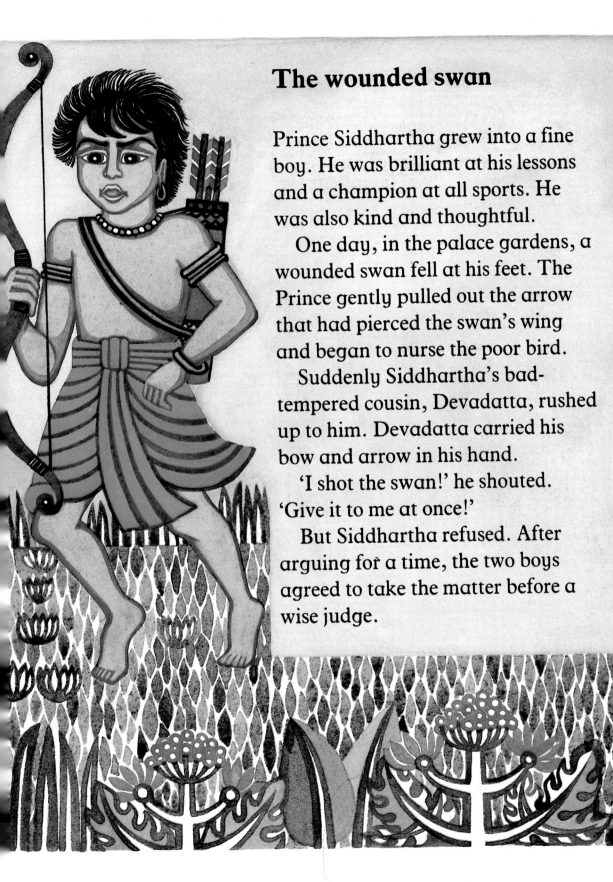

The wounded swan

Prince Siddhartha grew into a fine boy. He was brilliant at his lessons and a champion at all sports. He was also kind and thoughtful.

One day, in the palace gardens, a wounded swan fell at his feet. The Prince gently pulled out the arrow that had pierced the swan's wing and began to nurse the poor bird.

Suddenly Siddhartha's bad-tempered cousin, Devadatta, rushed up to him. Devadatta carried his bow and arrow in his hand.

'I shot the swan!' he shouted. 'Give it to me at once!'

But Siddhartha refused. After arguing for a time, the two boys agreed to take the matter before a wise judge.

15

The judge listened to what each of them had to say. He thought the matter over carefully for a long time. Finally he said: 'It is better to give life than to take it. The swan must therefore be yours, Siddhartha. Please take it . . .'

Siddhartha took the swan. Later, when it was completely better, he let it go free.

16

18

The Ploughing Festival

When he was seven years old, Prince Siddhartha was taken to the Ploughing Festival by his father. While King Suddhodana drove the great oxen that pulled the golden plough, the young Prince was left by himself beneath a rose-apple tree.

He did not watch the King plough the first furrow. Instead he half-closed his eyes and looked inside himself. There, on the surface of his mind, he could see a mass of thoughts, feelings, wishes and memories: all spinning away like a merry-go-round.

As he watched, however, his mind began to slow down. Then he saw in the depths of his mind a place that was calm and clear, like the waters of a deep, deep lake. When the others came back they were amazed to see him so still and peaceful.

'Why, he looks just like a little buddha!' someone exclaimed.

They all fell silent for they noticed that King Suddhodana was looking rather worried!

An end to suffering?

The years passed. Prince Siddhartha became a young man. He then married a beautiful princess named Yasodhara. Later, they had a young son themselves. They named him Rahula.

But now Prince Siddhartha started to become restless. He also wanted to know what life was like beyond the marble walls of his three splendid palaces.

So one day he asked his servant, Channa, to hitch the horses to his chariot and drive him to the nearest village. What he saw there on that day, and on the days following, completely changed his life.

On the first visit to the village, he saw an old man.

On the second visit, he saw a very sick man.

On the third visit, he saw a dead body being carried to a funeral.

Now, because of the sheltered way that King Suddhodana had brought him up, Prince Siddhartha had never seen these things before. He was deeply shocked.

'Why do people have to suffer like this?' he asked himself over and over again. 'Why? Why? Why . . .? Is there any way of putting an end to all this pain?'

Channa took him down to the village a fourth time. On that visit the Prince saw a man who had shaved all his hair off and wore a ragged robe of rough cloth.

'Who is he, Channa?' the Prince asked his servant.

'Oh, he's only an old holy man, Your Highness,' Channa replied. 'People like him live in lonely places and spend all their time thinking about very serious things.'

'And yet he seems strangely happy,' Prince Siddhartha said. 'Perhaps he's found a secret way of putting an end to suffering.'

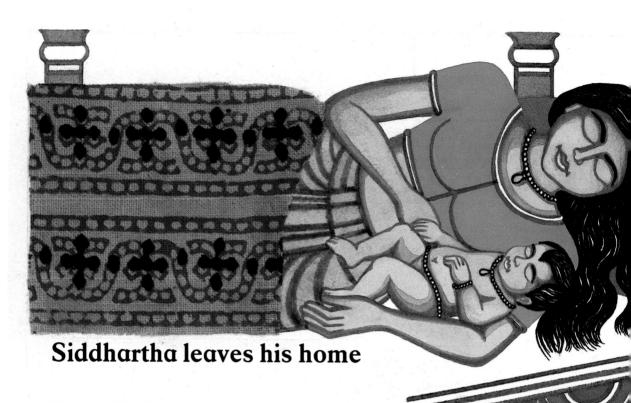

Siddhartha leaves his home

Prince Siddhartha was very unhappy. He kept thinking all the time about suffering. At last he decided that he would have to leave his palaces and become a homeless holy man himself in order to find out if pain and suffering could be brought to an end.

So one night he got up quietly and dressed. He felt very sad when he saw his wife and son sleeping there. He really did not want to leave them, but he knew that he could not stay. He wiped a tear from his eye and left.

27

Channa saddled the Prince's horse, Kanthaka. Then they rode to the river where his father's kingdom came to an end. There the Prince took off his rich silk robe and exchanged it for the ragged brown one of a holy man. He cut off his fine black hair too. Finally he took off all his rings and jewels and gave them to Channa.

'Here, Channa, please take these back to the palace with you. I will not need them any more,' the Prince said. 'Please take my horse Kanthaka home too.'

29

Channa began to cry bitterly. 'How can you do this, Your Highness?' he asked. 'How can you give everything up and go off and leave us? We all love you so much.'

'Please don't cry, Channa,' the Prince said softly. 'I hate to see people suffering. I want to find a way of ending suffering.'

'If you find a way, please promise that you'll come back and tell the rest of us about it,' Channa begged.

'I promise,' Siddhartha replied. 'Now please go back to the palace, my friend – quickly.'

Siddhartha searched the forests until
he found the wisest holy men of all.
They told him that if he treated his
body harshly, he would put an end
to suffering.

So Siddhartha lived in graveyards
among the dead. He slept on beds of
thorns. He burned in the heat of the
midday sun and he froze at night.
He also starved himself so that he
became almost as thin as a skeleton.

34

'But I still haven't managed to put an end to suffering,' he realized one day. 'And if I go on treating myself like this, I'll die before I find one.'

So he took a little food to give himself strength.

This really upset the other holy men in the forest. 'Siddhartha has taken to the easy life,' they grumbled – and they left him.

Alone and forsaken now, Prince Siddhartha sat down beneath the spreading branches of a great Bo tree.

'I'll stay here until I find what I'm searching for – even if I have to sit here until I die,' he promised himself faithfully.

Nirvana

Siddhartha now did again what he had done at the Ploughing Festival: he just lowered his eyelids and looked into his own mind. Soon he found that deep place where all was calm and clear. Then, gradually, he began to see that suffering is caused by craving. If we see something nice, we run after it. If we see something nasty, we push it away. Because of this we are never satisfied, never at peace . . .

38

There lived at this time a terrible demon named Mara who liked to see people suffering. When Mara saw what Siddhartha was doing, he began to get very worried.

'I must stop him – and fast!' he thought to himself.

During the night of the full moon in May, Mara tried all his tricks. He whipped up a mighty storm; he hurled thunderbolts down upon Siddhartha; he sent a great army of devils to frighten him. He even sent his beautiful daughters to try to persuade Siddhartha to give up.

But Siddhartha ignored it all. He just went on sitting quietly, looking into his mind. Then, towards dawn, he looked up and saw the morning star rise. At that moment he discovered what he had been looking for all along: a place in his own heart that was completely at peace. There was no craving there and no suffering or death either. The place he had found was called *Nirvana*.

The Awakened One

When he found *Nirvana*, Siddhartha felt like a man waking from a deep, deep sleep. He was then no longer Siddhartha, but the Buddha – 'The Awakened One'.

At first the Buddha did not really want to try and tell people what he had found out. He felt that it was too difficult for them to understand. Later, however, the great god Brahma Sahampati appeared before him and begged:

'Please teach us, *Bhante*. There are many people with just a little dust in their eyes. With some help from you, they may be able to see clearly too – and then they will also be free of suffering.'

42

The Buddha agreed. For the next forty-five years, he walked the hot and dusty roads of India, teaching all kinds of people the wise things that he had discovered. Some were ordinary people, who had homes and jobs and families. Other people, though, were prepared to give everything up in order to follow him. They became monks and nuns and lived very simple and good lives.

The fellowship of Buddhist monks and nuns is called the *Sangha*. It still exists today.

The Buddha did not forget his own
people. As he had promised Channa,
he did one day return to the
kingdom of King Suddhodana. By
then his fame had spread far and
wide, and all the people came out
eagerly to see the great teacher.

Naturally, the Buddha's close
relations were especially glad to see
him again. They had missed him
very much. But King Suddhodana
was rather upset when he saw his
son carrying a begging bowl around
his city. He felt that it was a great
disgrace – and he told the Buddha
so. The Buddha patiently explained
that it was his custom to eat only
food given to him by kind people.

'What do you mean, your custom?'
the King retorted. 'No member of my
family has ever had to beg for food.'

'That is true, Your Majesty,' the
Buddha agreed. 'But when I left the
royal family I took up the homeless
life. I now belong to the family of
wise men and buddhas.'

There was something very special about the Buddha now. Many of his close relations were deeply moved by the wonderful sense of peace they felt whenever they were near him. The Buddha's son, Rahula, and his step-brother, Nanda, became monks. And later his aunt, Prajapati, and his wife, Yasodara, became nuns.

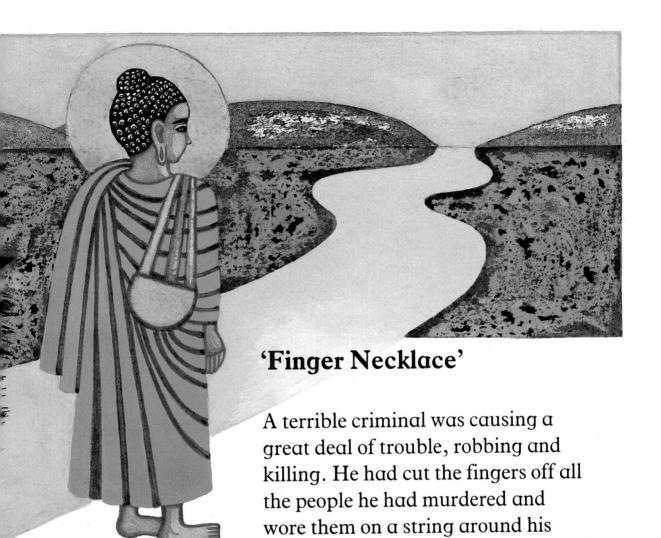

'Finger Necklace'

A terrible criminal was causing a
great deal of trouble, robbing and
killing. He had cut the fingers off all
the people he had murdered and
wore them on a string around his
neck. The people therefore called
him Angulimala, which means
'Finger Necklace.'

One day Angulimala caught sight
of the Buddha walking down a
lonely road by himself. 'Aha, a
monk!' the old villain chuckled to
himself. 'I'll make short work of
him!' Picking up his sword, he
began to chase the Buddha.

But no matter how fast Angulimala ran, he could not catch the Buddha. At last, tired and breathless, he cried out, 'Hey, monk, stop!'

'But I have stopped, Angulimala,' the Buddha replied quietly. 'I have stopped using violence. Isn't it time that you stopped too?'

These words touched the tiny pocket of goodness that remained in the bottom corner of Angulimala's black heart. At once, he flung away his sword and fell to his knees. Sobbing, he begged the Buddha to take him as one of his monks.

'Certainly,' the Buddha agreed without a moment's hesitation. 'But you must take off that awful necklace first!'

52

Kisagotami

An unhappy woman named Kisagotami one day visited the Buddha. She was crying and in her arms she carried the tiny body of a dead baby.

'Please give me some medicine that will bring my child back to life, *Bhante*,' she begged the Buddha.

The Buddha looked at the sad woman with kindly eyes. He knew that there was no medicine that could bring the child back to life. But he also knew that she was too upset to accept this. It was a difficult problem, so the Buddha thought about it for a few moments.

'I think I can help you,' he said. 'You must bring me one mustard seed – and that seed must come from a house in which no death has ever taken place.'

Kisagotami hurried away. She was sure that she would have no difficulty finding one mustard seed. But at every house she visited, the story was the same: someone had died there. One family had recently lost their old grandmother; another lady had lost her husband; a husband had lost his wife . . .

Later that day, Kisagotami returned to the Buddha. Gently she laid her dead child down at his feet.

'I see now that I am not alone in my great sadness,' she said. 'Death touches everyone sooner or later.'

'Bury your child, then, good lady,' the Buddha said. There were tears in his eyes, for his heart was full of loving kindness and he felt the pain and sadness of others as if they were his own.

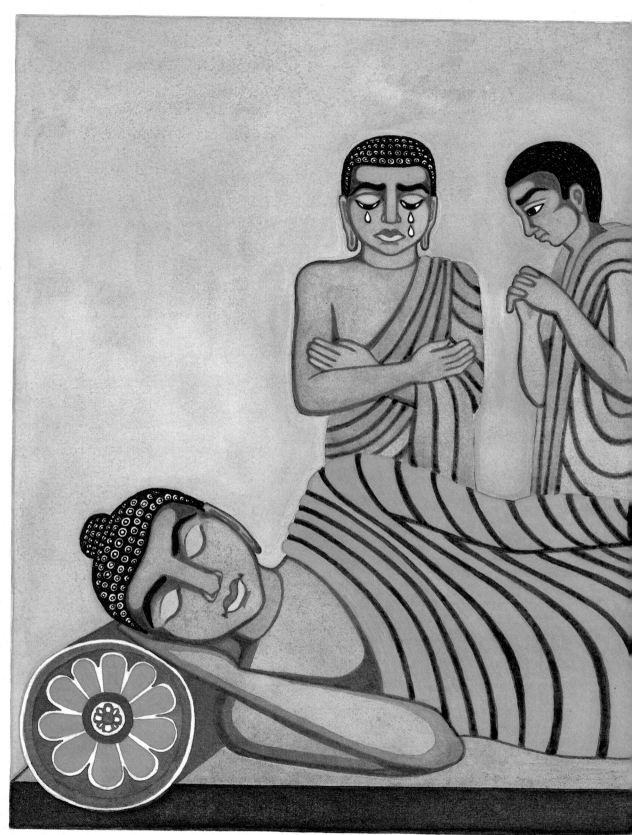

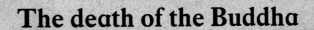

The death of the Buddha

The Buddha was an unusually kind and wise person, but he was neither a god nor a superman. He was human and, like all of us, he too had to die one day.

When he was about eighty years old he ate some food that had been poisoned. As he lay sick and dying, his followers gathered round him. They were all deeply upset and many were crying. The animals and birds were crying too, and so were the gods in the heavens. For a buddha, a truly Awakened One, comes into this world only once in thousands and thousands of years. There must, therefore, be great sadness everywhere at the hour of a buddha's death.

List of characters and places

Angulimala A terrible murderer who wore the fingers of his victims on a string around his neck. When he met the Buddha he changed his ways and became a monk.

Asita A fortune-teller who saw Prince Siddhartha shortly after his birth and predicted that he would either become a great emperor or a great religious teacher.

Brahma Sahampati The great god who persuaded the Buddha to teach people about his discovery of *Nirvana*.

Buddha Literally 'The Awakened One'. This is the title given to Prince Siddhartha when, at about the age of 35, he discovered the path to *Nirvana*, or 'The Deathless' (see also **Prince Siddhartha** below).

Channa Prince Siddhartha's groom.

Devadatta Prince Siddhartha's unpleasant cousin.

Himalaya The name means 'Abode of Snow' and refers to the great range of mountains that runs along the entire northern edge of the Indian sub-continent from Pakistan to Assam. It includes mounts Everest, Kanchenjunga, Makulu, Cho Oyo, Nanda Devi and other of the world's highest peaks.

Kisagotami The sad woman who asked the Buddha for medicine to bring her dead child back to life.

Lumbini Prince Siddhartha's birth-place.

Mara The wicked demon who tried to prevent Prince Siddhartha from finding *Nirvana*.

Maya, Queen Prince Siddhartha's mother.

Nanda Prince Siddhartha's step-brother. He joined the *Sangha* after Prince Siddhartha had found *Nirvana*.

Prajapati Prince Siddhartha's aunt.

Rahula The son of Prince Siddhartha and Princess Yasodhara.

Siddhartha, Prince Also known as Siddhartha Gautama. He lived in northern India about 2,500 years ago. He was greatly disturbed by the fact that human beings suffer in thousands of different ways. So, at about the age of 29, he gave up his royal inheritance to become a penniless holy man and look for a way to overcome suffering. After years of hard and painful struggle, he found that way. He then became the Buddha (see above).

Suddhodana, King The father of Prince Siddhartha. He was the ruler of a tiny kingdom situated at the foot of the Himalayan mountains in northern India.

Yasodhara, Princess The wife of Prince Siddhartha Gautama and the mother of his son, Rahula.

Glossary

Bhante   Literally 'Venerable Sir'. A respectful way to address a Buddhist monk.

Bo tree   The name given to the peepul tree (or sacred fig) by the Buddhists of India and Sri Lanka. It was under a tree of this kind that the Buddha is supposed to have found *Nirvana*. The traditional site of this event, at Bodh Gaya, is still the most important place of pilgrimage for Buddhists in India.

Buddhism   The religion that has grown up around the teachings of the Buddha. At first it spread through India but by the thirteenth century AD it had been wiped out there by the invasions of Prophet Muhammad's armies. It did not die out completely, however, because it spread south to Sri Lanka and other south-east Asian countries, and north to Tibet, Central Asia, China, Mongolia, Korea, and Japan. Buddhism is generally regarded as one of the five great religions of the world. It is becoming increasingly popular in Western countries.

Chariot   A light, two-wheeled cart pulled by horses.

Craving   A longing or strong desire for something.

Demon   An evil spirit.

Furrow   A long, deep trench cut into the soil by a plough.

Marble   A white stone which can be highly polished and which is often used to decorate fine buildings.

Nirvana   A peaceful state which each person can discover within themselves. There is no grasping there, no restlessness. Suffering cannot disturb it. Nor is it subject to death – so it may be called 'The Deathless'.

Sangha   The fellowship of Buddhist monks and nuns.

Textual note

The Pali Canon, the basic scriptures that recount what the Buddha himself actually taught, represent a vast body of literature. They are broadly divided into three sections or 'baskets' *(pitaka)*: the *Vinaya Pitaka* (the rules by which monks and nuns should live), the *Sutta Pitaka* (the dialogues or discourses of the Buddha) and the *Abhidhamma Pitaka* (the commentaries on the latter). These were not written down until about 300 or 400 years after the Buddha's death, but were until then memorized by certain monks and handed on by word of mouth.

These early scriptures do not contain an actual biography of the Buddha but frequent reference is made in passing to concrete events in his life. From these a 'life' may be pieced together. Biographies in the strict sense began to appear rather later, one of the first versions being Ashvaghosha's *Buddhacarita* or 'Acts of the Buddha' in the second century AD. Many others have appeared and in recent years there have been ones in English. Inevitably, modern scholars have debated the historical accuracy of the records of the Buddha's life that have been handed down to us.

Books to read

For Teachers
Bechert H. & Gombrich R. (eds), *The World of Buddhism* (Thames & Hudson, 1984)
Carrithers, Michael, *The Buddha* (Oxford, 1983)
Conze, Edward, *A Short History of Buddhism* (Allen & Unwin, 1982)
Humphreys, Christmas, *A Popular Dictionary of Buddhism* (Curzon Press, 1984)
Rahula, Walpola, *What the Buddha Taught* (Gordon Fraser, 1978)
Saddhatissa, H. *The Life of the Buddha* (Allen & Unwin, 1976)
Thomson, Garry, *Reflections on the Life of the Buddha* (Buddhist Society)

For younger readers
Ascott, Joan, *Our Buddhist Friends* (National Christian Education Council, 1978)
Bancroft, Anne *The Buddhist World* (Macdonald, 1984)
Barker, Carol, *Anada in Sri Lanka: A Story of Buddhism* (Hamish Hamilton, 1985)
Landaw, J., and Brooke, J., *Prince Siddhartha* (Wisdom, 1984)
Moran, Peggy, ed., *Buddhist Stories* (Privately published 1984, available from Westminister College, North Hinksey, Oxford OX2 9AT)
Patrick, Martha, *Buddhists and Buddhism* (Wayland, 1982)
Snelling, John, *Buddhism* (Wayland, 1986)
Snelling, John, *Buddhist Festivals* (Wayland, 1985)
Snelling, John, *Buddhist Stories* (Wayland, 1986)
Snelling, John, *Ten Buddhist Fables* (Buddhist Publication Group)

India Book House Education Trust also produces a number of good quality colour comic books in the *Amar Chitra Katha* series. Some of these retell various *Jataka* tales and Number 22 is about the life of the Buddha. Available in the UK from: Books from India, 45 Museum Street, London WC1. The Buddhist Society (58 Eccleston Square, London SW1V 1PH) represents all Buddhist traditions and publishes a wide range of printed material and cassette tapes.